FLAWED

SWEETIE FELCIE FERNANDES

INDIA • SINGAPORE • MALAYSIA

ISBN

Paperback 979-8-89699-970-6
Hardcase 979-8-89724-779-0

CONTENTS

ACKNOWLEDGEMENTS

Every Person That Has Walked Into My Life, Played a Role as They Touched My Soul, Thanking One or Two Would Do Them So Much Wrong, Hence I Thank Them All. And You My Lovely Readers Too…

I Bring Forth to You a Collection of Thoughts Which May Range from Light to Dark, Young to Old… Real-Unreal You'll Get To Know.

So Flip the Pages and Read Between the Lines for That's Where Reality Lies...

CARE SEEMS MILES AWAY

Care is not what I lack,

But I know not how to express it;

My trust you broke,

My heart you shattered,

Yet I choose to care…

A promise you made,

To be my guiding light;

Force me not to believe your deceit.

There is nothing you ever meant,

Not a single promise kept,

A second chance you lost,

Broke me through and through

Aloof I will be now,

For I fear to care again.

KNOCK MY DOOR ONCE MORE

Unaware was I of your pain,

Waiting, not knowing, would you return?

A messenger came my way,

The news of your suffering he whispered,

Worry filled my conscience,

Heart felt the pain,

For something I long to say,

My lips seemed sealed,

Words did not spill.

A sunset away was your return,

The moon making way for the sun.

So I ran with anguish in my heart;

A sudden thunder rumbled,

Reality knocked on my door,

When opened, I found a dream lost in snow.

FAIRYTALE

A perfect life I dream,

A beauty sleep I plead,

Life so cruel,

I wish could heal.

A tiny girl who dreamed,

For endless loving streams,

All dried and gone into,

A heartless beam.

Life makes no sense,

Weird paths I cross,

A picture perfect view,

Can it be only untrue?

Little girl grew up,

For her prince she awaits,

Days pass by,

Not a soul in sight.

Days turn into years,

Old age traps her in,

Close to the end,

Locked up in her cell.

Hence they say:

"A Happy Ending Is All A Fairytale"

CAN'T BREAK A BROKEN HEART

Now I have grown up all strong,

Every expectation gone wrong;

You can't break a broken heart,

You can't break what's broken apart;

The pieces have been washed away,

To a place with no Light or Day,

In an ocean filled with hate.

BLIND LOVE

A flower bloomed in my heart,

Restless was I when far apart,

Blessed I felt when close to you,

Hell it seemed when away you went.

Music played at the sight of you,

Honey coated words flowed endlessly,

Tender joy that you gave me so true,

My life was a magical rainbow without a clue.

Flaws in you I could not see,

Wrong things looked so right,

Feelings were wrapped in a bubble of joy,

For it to break I did not want.

Blindly followed your path my love,

Did not hesitate to sacrifice my heart,

Happy I always wanted you to be,

Forgave you for the day you hurt me.

We may never cross paths again,

But respect for you isn't lost yet,

Heart I cannot teach to beat,

For it choose you to bleed.

THE EVIL OF THE EYE

Conflict surrounded her soul,

Every Evil that she saw,

Evoked a thought,

A thought of worshipping Satan deep within.

Devil played tricks on her mind,

God dominated her soul.

The Almighty protected her from harm,

While the Devil envied her Charm.

Eternity in Heaven,

Or Fire in Hell did she choose?

Who was she?

To worship whom had she come?

Different were her ways;

A Child of Satan being raised

Or a Sheep gone astray.

BLEEDING LOVE

The look on his face,

The love in his eyes,

Makes me lose my mind,

Emotions I cannot hide,

I love him more than life.

Thorns pierce my heart,

Every drop of my blood his name imprinted.

Peaceful he seemed,

But the hurt inside him, was so extreme.

His voice firm and strong,

Melted away any wrong,

In my heart he lived,

A part of him I would forever be,

Every step I would follow,

Every breath I would live.

This smile will never leave my face,

For even pain has a joy of its own.

As he turns the chapters of his life,

I stand here,

My wound fresh as his story lives,

The flames of my love vanish.

SHADES OF THE SUN

Watching the sunset with you by my side,

Was a wonderful feeling that I couldn't hide,

And the fire blazing in your eyes,

As the sun minimized,

It was rocket science I couldn't define.

You struck my heart as the rays of the sun declined,

Red, Orange, Yellow, I didn't mind.

For like our fingers,

Feelings were also intertwined.

HIM

He found perfection in my imperfections,

He thought my smile was one in a million,

He loved me beyond imagination,

He was shattered when I crushed his jubilation.

He was yet a dear friend to me,

He could see hope for eternity,

He wanted to take away all my pain,

He was in denial when I crushed him all over
again.

He was now happy with her,

He then ended his relationship with laughter,

He asked me to marry him in the near future,

He was headed into a disaster.

He then got all strong,
He kept me hanging all along,
He was scared that I would flee,
He then hurt me ruthlessly.

He said that we couldn't be,
He said that we were history,
He left me with a mystery,
He wrecked me, left me lost and lonely.

He turned the tables,
He broke the promises he made,
He looked at me from a distance,
He kept breaking me at every instance.

He now fell in love with another her,
He wanted to make it happen all along,
He gave her his all, that I envied,
He pushed me away as she led his way.

He didn't need me now, for he had her,

He then gave me the news of the agony caused by her,

He asked if that's how I had felt,

He felt defeated, I didn't sympathize.

He wasn't ready; at least that's what I felt,

He was weeping as I pretended to care,

He looked into my eyes; revenge was all I felt,

He felt the shock as I walked out on him again.

He was incharge now, as strong as a rock,

He despised me; stayed away from my touch,

He made me feel like I was poison to his heart,

He loathes for me now for I didn't bid goodbye.

Now I feel wrong for playing charades with his heart,

Now I can't see him stepping into the dark

Now I want to assure him that it's going to be alright,

But now is too late, for this Him is a Falcon in the dark.

CHAPEL OF GREED

She does all that is asked of her

She feels more than one can think

She is trapped in a cube of sadness

She is a slave of their greed

She loathes every moment of her being

She hides under the mask of happiness

She has felt more hate than love

She longs for love from her maker

She isn't understood by them

She feeds the blazing fire within

She is her only hope

She needs an escape from her reality

She seeks for a rescuer

She instead discovers her new identity

In the Chapel of Greed.

SOUL MATES

A bond more precious than love.

An understanding even words cannot convey.

Unspoken feelings our eyes express.

Silent presence soothes our souls.

Heartache stopped us from taking risks.

Countless kisses we missed.

A loving touch could heal another.

So much for not wanting to lose him forever.

Every passing moment was proof,

That we were meant to be.

And then by the riverside

He held me with gentle hands

His soft eyes whispering,

"We really are Soul mates, aren't we?"

GYPSY BOND

They met in the midst of life's crisis

Both wounded beyond the healing eye

Life wasn't all Unicorns for them

Familiarity tagged along with the pair

Endless chatter's got them awestruck

Dogging the evil world they bonded

As cloaked travelers in a ship of suspended time

Persistent foreplay had them reaching out for the
other

Physical intimacy wrapped them in a spell

With their heart's set on different souls

They found solace in this Gypsy Bond.

SHE HAD TO SURVIVE

Her heart had gone cold

People asked her why?

How could she have explained to them?

Her every cry…

They would not empathize.

They would only criticize.

Shutting out was

The only thing she could visualize

Hence now emotionless she scrutinized.

Everything she did was to fill her selfish heart

I really would not blame her,

This world is a cruel place

And she had to Survive.

HEALING

I am healing at my own pace

There is no hurry

Everyone heals differently

Maybe not completely.

This process is challenging

Takes effort for one to be bold enough

Decision making is taxing

Fear of change will forever be there

Do I trust myself to finally move on?

To take a leap of faith?

It cannot get worse.

It gets tiring but I believe I can heal.

A DAUGHTER, NOT HER FATHER'S PRINCESS

A father so cruel,

The devil's minion.

A sadist you are,

To find pleasure in pain.

Words bitter you say,

For you kill more than heal.

Snakes are gentler,

For you are the poison.

Respect you don't deserve,

For a disgrace to fathers you are.

A failure to man you are,

My world collapsed the day I was born.

For you were my father,

Before I was born.

Thirst for love is what I had,

But hate is all I received.

A being as vile as you,

Even vultures won't eat your flesh.

A hug is what I asked,

But a scar is what you gave.

Blame me not now,

Rude is what I will be.

I never was loved,

Care seemed miles away.

A hollow stone you've made me,

Don't think that I will bother,

A second chance you will never get.

Locked up are all my feelings,

A glimpse of which you won't have.

Try as much as you may,

Unmoving I will be.

The day you die,

My freedom I will rejoice.

AND MY PRINCE VANISHED

He came into my life like a breath of fresh air.

Our eyes met, there were sparks.

My cheeks so red that even red would shy away.

Heart racing at a rhythm unknown.

Even in a crowd his eyes could find me.

He would walk towards me without shifting his gaze.

So many nothings to share;

Words spoken had no meaning but made perfect sense.

But everything perfect has an ultimatum.

Mistakes were made, pride got in the way.

Only an apology could fix the broken relationship.

Conversations turned into heartbreaking silence.

From being so close to being perfect strangers.

And just as he came, my Prince vanished.

WILL I GROW TO LOVE YOU?

Exhausted I fall into your arms.

You kiss it away with your charm.

Even when tiredness takes over.

I want you to claim me as yours.

I offer myself to you, but you know better.

And what do I know of the pain I am going to experience?

Its foreign territory to me.

And there is no one to protect my heart, it lays shattered like glass.

The pain will subside, I assure you.

But you do not go around mending hearts.

You know that I do not love you, nor did I ever.

But will I grow to love you?
This uncertainty is devastating.

UNOPENED WINE BOTTLES

Wine bottles lie in my cupboard unopened.

I pictured a candlelight dinner.

I would cook you steak and bake you chocolate
cake.

Sip our wine while we stare in each other's eyes

And then you say something funny, makes me
laugh.

You find that cute, you come close

Hold my face, kiss me because you cannot help
yourself.

We make love by the fire place.

You stroke my hair as you tell me you love me.

We gaze at the stars wrapped into each other's
arms.

Wake up next morning with a smile on our face.

But those wine bottles lie in my cupboard
unopened.

You do not let me share them with any other
person.

Nor do you show up with a corkscrew.

FADE AWAY

Now I lie wide awake in my bed

Thinking about all those happy moments.

Remembering the time when you made me smile.

Your charming ways caught my attention.

Ignoring the pain caused by my prior heartbreak

I had let myself be vulnerable again.

I gave you the right to hurt me.

Oh which you truly did.

Now it hurts worse than before

And this time I do not know if there is coming back
from it.

So I am asking you,

Tear my heart up let the pain fade away.

FIRE

A curly mess with a fire blazing within.

A fire so wild, will turn you to ash.

But yet you choose to tease it

In the hopes of taming

What cannot be tamed.

RELATIONSHIP

I want those long drives

I want those small fights

I want those silly late night talks

I want those heart aching cries

I want those movie dates

I want those blue days

I want those kisses in the rain

I want those jealousy pang

I want those cuddles

I want those crazy outbreaks

I want those makeup sessions

I want those silly time offs

I want my dreams to come true

I want some to be crushed

I want to kiss you

I want to punch you

I want to make love with you

I want to argue with you

I want that feeling of being safe

I want some unpleasant surprises

I want those motivational talks

I want those random meltdowns

I want you to love me

But life does not always give us what we want,
does it?

BROKEN

I am broken beyond repair.

I know I am not easy to love.

I am hurting so I hurt you.

I hurt you so that I do not get hurt.

I know I am wounded, selfish.

I have been so damaged.

I don't believe you when you say you love me.

I run away when things start to get real.

I am that dark cloud that ruins a sunny day.

I am what I am.

But do you have the patience to try?

CALM TO MY STROM

Talking to you is a soothing feeling.

It heals me at a faster pace.

You are the definition of cheesy.

Who calms my vibrant personality.

I need a constant more than anything right now.

So much for my abandonment issues.

You are so giving in this selfish world.

I've been existing for so long,

You give me reason to live.

Changed this mask into true happiness.

UNSETTLING MORNINGS

That morning when you wake up
And you have this unsettling feeling.
Like something bad is ought to come
And nothing seems alright.

All by yourself you just sit there
And stare at the wall for hours.
So many heart aching thoughts
And senseless loud cries.

You are there just waiting,
Waiting for something to go wrong.
But then you turn around
And see the sun shine.

IT HURTS

He says things to me that get me all confused.

Making me feel I actually mean something to him.

And then in a heartbeat he kills that hope.

He is not allowed to do that!

He is not allowed to toy with my feelings!

Nor should I let him affect me like that.

And I am really trying but it hurts.

I want to cry but then again, I have no right to.

It is not like he promised me hugs and roses.

But when he looks at me like that

And makes it obvious to other's that I am his,

It hurts…

PHOTOGRAPH

Looking back at the Photograph,

Everything made sense.

Now I could see that,

He held my hand

But looked into her eyes.

CHOICE

We were each other's second choice,

Yet together we made the best voice,

In the end Friend's made better lovers.

FORBIDDEN LOVE

A strong undying passion for love,

Made me explore beyond the boundaries of ice,

Played hide and seek with the snowflakes,

Hopped onto a glacier with pride.

Swan across oceans, found warmth,

Felt an unknown feeling called comfort,

Melting into the lit spark,

The heart gave me a shrill or felt the thrill?

Even as the flame heightened;

And everything turned blur,

There was one thing yet so clear,

That was forbidden love my dear.

BOOKWORM

She was seated across my table,

A total stranger I would say.

A cup of coffee we bonded over,

Her smile had a childish play.

Innocence danced around her halo,

Did not know her charm would slay.

The mischief in her eyes,

Her witty replies, took me by surprise,

Unaware, she left a mark,

That could not be washed away.

A bookworm with her secrets made of clay.

HIDE AWAY

When I care about someone,

I shut myself out.

Being so vulnerable makes me angry.

I am so used to being strong,

That I hate when someone can affect me,

Even though I have the intuition,

That there is something this time around.

Instead, I hideaway in my cave.

I am a mess, I have always been one,

I need to pick myself up and focus,

And build up courage to face what is coming next.

So badly that I need to switch my Humanity off.

BREAK MY WALL

I have not cried in years,

I have become cold I say.

I do not let anyone in,

I keep everyone at bay,

People walk away.

And the feeling of being left behind is devastating.

I am scared to scare them away with my sadness.

It scares me not to belong anywhere.

And the anger building inside me will destroy me.

But why am I so angry?

Is it the thought of being so worthless?

There is nothing but emptiness inside me.

I need someone to find a way to break my wall.

Because I am willing to be fixed.

LOST AT SEA IN THIS WICKED WORLD

A passing canoe with a friendly face,

Offers to help reach across,

Tells a tale of gruesome pain,

Stranger gains a companion,

Companion confided in a moment

Stranger felt like family.

A storm was coming their way,

A ship in near sight,

Stranger flashes a red light,

A rope ladder released,

Stranger climbs, reaches the top

And cuts the ladder off.

Companion left at sea,

Knowing not the art of swimming,

Confused at the strangers change of heart,

The selfishness caused alarm,

Companion could see clearly now,

A friendly face can be the enemy.

SOME DAY IT WILL BE OURS

A bubble popping out of her perfect lips,

Those little brown eyes still asleep,

The innocence on her face,

In my arms at peace,

With the little white dress, she looked angelic.

The curl over her eyes,

And the heartwarming smile,

Even her cry so pure,

I felt this pull in my chest,

As he held us both in his arms,

Whispering in my ears,

"Some day it will be ours."

LUCIFER

And then he just walks in,

With his captivating gaze,

Asking for my hand,

With his devilish play,

I give in like some lovesick fool,

He pulls me close,

And dances to a rhythm from hell;

We tango till dawn,

The sky blush red,

His mask has fallen off,

But I am not scared.

I look up,

Charmed by his scared face,

Lost in his blazing dark eyes,

His lips meet mine,

Smirking as my heart beats,

And that's when I knew,

I was his muse,

Only his to love,

And only his to kill.

SERENITY

I look up at the clear sky,

Which now, hides behind the rain clouds,

And the leaves dance at its own tune,

While the wind plays a melody;

Amidst the sound of the water gushing,

A bug crawls over my skin,

While the birds fly majestically,

I feel the fish nibble on my toes,

Silent cries of the wild they say,

Little droplets on the marble stone,

The smell of nature fills the air,

Soothes my storm,

And in all of life's turmoil,

I wondered, if this is it,

If this is serenity.

FLAWED

We met, sparks lit, loved bloomed,

All was good but I could see the gloom,

Cause suddenly,

My speech didn't say obedience,

My clothes were ugly,

My footwear wasn't appropriate,

My behaviour wasn't lady like,

My curls were less curly,

My income was less,

My family was a disaster,

My body was a mess,

I get it,

Everything about me wasn't perfect,

Still isn't perfect,

But is anyone perfect?

I thought love meant acceptance.

Even with all the abuse,

I understood and compromised,

In between those constant tears,

There used to be an occasional smile.

Trauma bond much?

One day I spoke my truth,

Didn't know the truth would result in,

More abuse, more lies,

Playing on my vulnerability,

Manipulating my actions,

Made a mockery of my emotions,

Threatened my life,

And then played the victim,

But even on this grey day,

I picked up the broken pieces,

Stood with my head held up high,

Flawed, with hope in my eyes.

HUMAN CATASTROPHE

I look at you now and see a boy,

Longing to be a man,

Entrapped in denial,

With hypocrisy on a bender.

I thought there was change,

But I see things more clearly,

Age didn't define maturity,

Nor did it intrigue your curiosity.

Countless rock-solid opinions,

No legit resolutions,

Constantly playing the victim,

With no accountability for your actions.

Portraying cowardly behaviour as strength,

Thinking that isn't supported by logic,

Running away from responsibility,

Oh boy, karmas got you in a loop.

Unhappiness encircles you,

Anger issues lead to destruction,

A lot of lies and attempts of manipulation,

Insensitivity to physical violence,

Oh, such toxic energy,

Should one even feel bad for such a Human
Catastrophe?

SOMETHING MORE

It's been years now,

We have seen each other grow,

We laugh, we cry,

Never leave each other's side.

The touch feels so safe,

Even silence brings comfort,

No drama, no stress,

Everything just falls into place.

This feeling won't leave me,

Do we belong?

But it's too platonic,

And how do we go on,

To be something more?

Honestly, I don't know,

If these questions play on your mind,

Or is it just me?

Longing for something more.

REMEMBER ME

You sit and play me some music,

Flip through those random pages,

Making me laugh till I cry,

Oh, such happy times.

Humour is always your escape,

Singing even when you can't,

Dancing with two left feet,

Oh, live a little you say.

You always have a way,

To make everything brighter,

Even when you are not here,

Oh, the distance didn't make a difference.

We are inseparable now,

But what does the future hold?

When you find your match,

Would I be a long-lost memory?

Or would you remember me?

YOU BUILD FROM THERE

When you truly love someone,

And the one you love walks all over you,

Especially when you need that love the most,

It breaks you,

And you do some stupid things,

But that doesn't define you.

You were hurt and impulsive,

Once the blindfold drops,

You see you were blaming yourself for someone,

Who didn't deserve you,

And you build from there.

DEAR CHILDREN

Sometimes we forget all the hardships our parents
went through to raise us,

Regardless of their personality,

We should be grateful,

And treat them right in their old-age,

But instead, some cause so much hinderance,

That they affect their mental peace,

In the time they need us the most,

We shouldn't forget what goes around comes
around,

And then all we are left with is regret.

Be nice now it will come back.

CHER FRÈRE

I looked at your eager set of eyes,

When you held me in your arms,

I snuggled in, you comforted me,

But then gave me a knock on my head.

The little pranks you played,

Sometimes it went a little too far,

And you would tell me not to fret,

Cause you didn't wanna get caught.

You gave me the world,

What a big price I paid,

You said I was your baby sis,

And then called me a harlot.

You said you would protect me,
But you threw me to the wolfs,
All I want is peace Cher Frere,
Hope your glasses of Greed fall off.

You are being so reckless,
You are hurting your own,
You treated me like a princess,
And then sold me to the Devil.

BIRTHDAY BLUES

It's December, my birthday month,

But the child celebrating in me is dead.

I loved Christmas celebrations too,

But now it all just seems pointless.

Is this what growing up feels like?

Or is it just all the trauma haunting me?

Besides a few childhood blurs,

And bad birthday memories,

Surrounded by a dysfunctional family,

Am I just scared to be happy?

I would have got excited hoping this year is it,

When I would be treated right,

But the trauma doesn't leave me,

Of being treated like shit over and over,

Cause it had to be about him and not me,

Getting older, but things are only getting worse.

I still hope it's different this year,

And the joy of Christmas does find me,

This birthday I hope for peace,

And to finally be hopelessly happy.

OUR CREATOR CONTROLS THY NATURE

Infants of Thy Gentle Stream,

Flowing in Thy Love Insane:

Remember Thy Creator,

For He Controls Thy Nature.

Youth of Thy Burning Fire,

Spreads Upon Thy Universe Filled With Desire:

Remember Thy Creator,

For He Controls Thy Nature.

Elders Boast Thy Fire,

For Thy Winds Are What They Hire:

Remember Thy Creator,

For He Controls Thy Nature.

RING OF PEACE

Spirit on Earth,

White as Snow.

Blood so Pure,

We let it Glow.

Silent is the World,

Shines its Glory.

No more War,

Motto is Harmony.

In the Eyes of the Dove,

The Universe we see.

Innocence of a Child,

In our Heart we Glee.

A Crown of Thorns,

Sacrifice Overflowed.

The rays of the Sun,

A new Crown we impose.

The Trinity it belongs to,

Placed after Thee.

Great wonders Peace can do,
To you and to me.
Violence so Wrong,
Weak to Strong.
Wounds bleeding Red,
People Fred.
Sand slips away,
May it be Black, Brown or White!
In Heaven; the Promised Land.
Equal are they,

A Blind man will see.
A Deaf man will hear.
A Dumb man will speak.
Miracles do happen,
We ought to Believe.

CAN YOU TELL A LIE WHEN YOU SPEAK THE TRUTH?

Truth so pure,

A spear you endure.

A thousand hearts you break,

A million souls you save.

A crow you see,

A dove you seek.

A simple lie,

Complicate the life.

Harsh a truth,

Leads to paradise.

Sound no wrong,

Feel no right.

Yet is it true,

That people lie?

It makes no sense,

To tell a lie.

When truth glorifies.

Harm it may not cause,

At the present time,

But a land may slide

As guilt makes its way.

True can be false if delayed,

False can be true if the game is well played,

When truth and lie unite,

The Universe of reality will collide.

DREAM UNIVERSE DREAM

Live your dream,

Don't be scared,

You got a second chance,

I wish I had.

Rocks will melt,

But won't your wait,

Flowers will speak,

Your dreams won't sink

Take a step before it's too late.

The dead it can boost,

The poor it can rule,

The rich it can burn,

For dreams come true,

Must Believe You.

PUNISHED FOR LIFE

Crime unforgettable you committed,

The right to decide was not in your power,

Who were you to end one's life?

Eyes you laid upon a juvenile,

Touched her, Why? Why?

Innocent Virgin you bedded,

Didn't you hear her cry?

By law should you hang?

Or be sliced apart?

No right god has given us,

For even Mercy Killing is not a part.

Shameful it is why you survive.

But karma will seek revenge,

Painful will be your death,

Embarrassment will rule your life,

Guilt will tear you apart;

Belongingness you will long for,

But cruel will be the loneliness that you receive.

Even your shadow will leave your side;

For killing doesn't give you Pride.

BREAK THE CHAINS AND SET FREE THE HUMAN RACE

Human race they did belong to,

But like animal's they were treated them,

Pets seemed at mercy,

But they were not,

Colour bias so not fair,

Heaven above did not care.

Tortured they were

But they complained not,

Suffering they were chained to,

Respect they received not.

Thorns they walked on,

Slaves they were treated as,

Cuts and scars they were gifted,

Clothes were torn, food deprived,

Bombs were thrown upon their lives.

By something known as Humanity.

A spark they waited for,

To light up their heart,

The world they awaited,

To be worth the while,

Eyes glowed in the dark,

But when would the sun shine?

A bed of rocks did they sleep on,

But yet the Lord they worshipped,

Holy men were they,

To see hope in darkness.

Life was tolerable,

After blood was shed.

Freedom they got,

But was it real?

Were they fed?

He led the battle,

Struggle for freedom ensured.

Slow was the pace,

But free was the race.

Away from all humiliation,

A bed of roses given.

As same is the flesh,

As same is the blood,

Colourful is the world,

Distinction should not prevail;

For you and I are both human in the end.

LONELY HUNTER

Tears roll down my check,

When thoughts are so bleak,

Answers my mind seek,

Yet the heart pretends to be so sleek.

And when black and white,

Hid behind the clock,

With no place to go,

I took the lonely path,

Hunting for my better half,

But the road had no end.

I found myself wandering about in a circle with no
escape.

BLUE WATERS

Blue waters as dangerous as it can be,

Dolphin's creators of melody,

Man raids their privacy,

How cruel can the world be?

Peaceful speech the ocean has,

Marine studies a noisy mess,

No peace, no harmony,

How cruel can the world be?

Money talks, the water walks,

The water kingdom we have lost,

Toxic waste and drainage pipes,

Cruelty within us shines.

UNCERTAINTY

The uncertainty in life is commendable,

What's there now may seek existence tomorrow,

Some may be gone away in a blink,

Overthinking about the future is worrisome.

The past will tap into our conscious often,

But our approbation should stay in the present,

Take risks like there is no tomorrow,

Living surpasses existing;

Fear empowers taking away our kingdom,

So many stories wrecked,

So many unwritten,

Sorrow envelopes us,

Keeping us at bay,

Attachment plucked. Burned alive;

Blessed is he who finds a way in Uncertainty.

HAPPY EVER AFTER

Wearing a big sparkly white dress,
I walked towards the altar,
There he was with a goofy grin on his face,
In that moment I was happy.

A year down the line my happiness faded,
His grin scared me now,
His touch always left a scar,
My dress covered every inch of my body,
Makeup concealed the blues,
In that moment I felt helpless.

I loved him too much,
I told myself, this won't last forever,
He wasn't always like this,
Things would get better,
I would have my happy ever after,
In that moment I had hope.

Some more time passed, things got worse,
My delusions were clearing up,
I was running out of empathy,
The lows were overpowering the highs,
I decided to walk away from this brutality,
In that moment I felt free.

It wasn't easy, but my tears were drying up,
My smile was more genuine now,
The trauma started fading,
I realized it's the small goals that mattered,
I learned to love myself,
In that moment I was my happy ever after.

www.ingramcontent.com/pod-product-compliance
Lightning Source LLC
Chambersburg PA
CBHW031458150726
47990CB00007B/2806